SERMON OUTLINES
FOR
FUNERALS

2

SERMON OUTLINES
FOR
FUNERALS
2

C.W. Keiningham

BAKER BOOK HOUSE
Grand Rapids, Michigan 49516

ISBN: 0-8010-5493-1

Sixth printing, April 1998

Printed in the United States of America

For information about academic books, resources for Christian
leaders, and all new releases available from Baker Book House,
visit our web site:
http://www.bakerbooks.com/

Contents

1

Elderly Woman
Genesis 23:1, 2

I. The Years of Her Life
A. Sarah's years were said to be 127
   1. Her life cannot be measured in years
     a. Jesus lived only about thirty-three years
     b. Life is often measured by accomplishments
   2. Her life was a long series of experiences
     a. Like so many links in a chain
     b. Like many frames that make up a movie
B. The deceased lived a long life
   1. Our memory is not of the many years
   2. Our memory is of the many individual experiences

II. The End of Her Life
A. Sarah died in Kirjatharba
   1. Her earthly life came to an end
     a. Her opportunities and activities ended
     b. The human history of Sarah concluded
   2. Her personal existence did not end
B. Death is not the end of life—Phil. 1:23
   1. It is the end of one's earthly experiences
   2. There is life beyond that—John 11:25
   3. There is resurrection life in the future—1 Thess. 4
C. We do not gather to mark the end of a life but to recall that life

III. The Feelings About Her Life
A. Abraham came to mourn and weep
   1. Because of her value to him
   2. Because of his feelings for her
B. We have gathered for a memorial
   1. Because she was of great value to us
   2. Because of our respect and feelings for her
C. More important are God's feelings—Matt. 25:21

2

A Spiritual Paradox
Romans 8:6

I. Some Are Dead Before They Die
  A. Those who have not been saved
     1. They are dead in sins—Eph. 2:1
     2. Man is a threefold creature
        a. He is body—world consciousness
        b. He is soul—self consciousness
        c. He is spirit—God consciousness
     3. An unsaved person is spiritually dead
        a. He has no God-consciousness
        b. He has no spiritual life—1 Cor. 2:14
  B. Those who are carnally minded
     1. This is living after the flesh—Rom. 8:13a
     2. This is a Christian who is worldly
        a. Who is preoccupied with worldly affairs
        b. The Parable of the Sower—Mark 4:18, 19

II. Some Are Alive After They Die
  A. Those who have been saved
     1. They are dead with Christ—2 Tim. 2:11
     2. They are believers in Christ—John 11:25
     3. They shall never perish—John 10:28
     4. They have Christ within—Rom. 8:10
  B. Those who are spiritually minded
     1. Who have had their minds renewed—Rom. 12:2
     2. Who are walking in the Spirit—Rom. 8:13b
     3. Whose lives are hid with Christ—Col. 3:3

III. The Resurrection of the Dead
  A. Some will rise to eternal life—1 Thess. 4:17
  B. Some will rise to judgment—Rev. 20:11–15

3

Sleep of Death
Psalm 4:8

People have different attitudes toward death.
Christians should be serene about it.

I. God's Children Lie Down in Peace
A. They are submissive to God's will
1. They are ready to live or die—Acts 21:13
2. They have peace about death—text
B. They have concluded God's work assignment
1. Everyone has a work to do in life
2. Everyone remains until his work is done
   a. Peter in jail—Acts 12:7–10
   b. When it is finished, we lie down
C. They have finished their course—2 Tim. 4:7

II. God's Children Sleep
A. Death is not a horrible happening
1. It is a necessary transition—2 Cor. 15:50
2. It is a natural journey—Ps. 23:4a
B. Death is described as like physical sleep
1. The weary rest from their labors—Eccles. 5:12a
2. The sick escape from their illnesses—Rev. 21:4
3. The sad and sorrowing find joy—Rev. 21:4
4. The hurting find relief from pain—Rev. 21:4
5. The body waits for his coming—1 Thess. 4:16, 17

III. God's Children Dwell in Safety
A. The promise of Jesus—John 10:27–30
B. The angels are on guard—Jude 9 and Matt. 18:10
C. The angels are on duty—Luke 16:22 and Matt. 28:2
D. God himself watches over them—Ps. 23:4b

4

The Homecoming
Genesis 49:28–33

Death is likened to gathering one's feet into bed.

"Thanatopsis" by William Cullen Bryant.

"Approach thy grave like one who wraps the drapery of his couch about him and lies down to pleasant dreams."

I. Our Spirit Is Gathered with the Living
    A. "I am to be gathered unto my people"—(v. 29)
        1. Abraham, Sarah, Isaac, Rebekah and Leah—(v. 31)
        2. Jacob did not consider these dead
    B. Death is a gathering to the living
        1. The dead in Christ are with God—1 Thess. 4:14
        2. Death is like a homecoming at church
        3. Death is like a family reunion

II. Our Body Is Gathered with the Buried
    A. ". . . bury me with my fathers"—(v. 29)
        1. This was more sentimental than spiritual
        2. This was the result of close family ties
    B. Family plots are as common today as in the past
        1. We desire to be buried with our family
        2. Some are not able to be buried together
        3. The resurrection will solve this problem—1 Thess. 4:17

III. Our Family Is Gathered for the Parting
    A. A great company gathered—Gen. 50:7, 8
        1. Jacob's name had been changed to Israel
        2. Jacob was the father of the twelve tribes
        3. Jacob was a famous and revered man
    B. Some are not as famous and well known
        1. Our influence extends farther than we think
        2. We are gathered here for the parting
        3. Let it be a celebration—a homecoming

5

Death and God's Plan
Genesis 50:22-26

Joseph was a great, great grandfather.

He had two sons—Ephraim and Manasseh.

He saw three generations of Ephraim's children (v. 23).

He saw two generations of Manasseh's children v. 23).

I. Joseph Knew Death Was Coming
  A. Notice his words "I die" in verse 24
    1. This meant he would be leaving them
    2. This meant he would not be there to guide them
  B. People often sense when death is near—2 Tim. 4:6
    1. They even reach a point of acceptance
    2. This is part of God's provision for us

II. Joseph Knew God's Plan Would Continue
  A. His absence would not end the plan
    1. "God will surely visit and bring you out" (v. 24).
    2. "God will surely bring you to your possession" (v. 24).
  B. He wanted to be a part of it even after death
    1. His life had been dedicated to God's plan
    2. He wanted his bones carried out with them
  C. Everyone should desire to be a part of God's plan
    1. To find God's calling for his life
    2. To make his contribution to that plan

III. Joseph Died and Was Prepared
  A. He was embalmed and placed in a coffin (v. 26)
    1. This was an act of respect for him then
    2. This is still an act of respect today
  B. His knowledge of God and his plan was correct
    1. God did deliver them from Egypt
    2. God did bring them into the promised land
    3. Joseph's bones were buried there—Josh. 24:32
  C. Death is made easier by a knowledge of God's plan

6

Meeting with God
Exodus 3:4

Moses had a meeting with God.
Moses' life was never the same.

I. Not All Meetings with God Are Alike
  A. Because people and circumstances are different
  B. Because needs and callings are different
  C. Two things are the same in all meetings
    1. God initiates the meeting—John 3:16
    2. God's purpose is always the same
      a. He is trying to enter our lives—Rev. 3:20
      b. He is trying to prepare us for eternity

II. Not All Uncertainties Are Answered
  A. God didn't reveal everything to Moses
  B. Some are always asking why, how, or what
  C. Real faith doesn't require all the answers
    1. Faith follows even in darkness
    2. Faith follows even in confusion
    3. Faith follows even in suffering

III. Meetings with God Give a Different Point of View
  A. Moses' attitude changed after his meeting with God
  B. Life's troubles seem too much for us sometimes
    1. It seems we are bound for defeat
    2. It seems that too much is expected of us
  C. God gives us a different outlook—perspective
    1. We see life from his point-of-view
    2. Problems don't seem nearly so bad from there

IV. Meetings with God Are Important in Life
  A. We need God in charge of our lives
  B. We need God in charge of our eternities

7

Tragic Death of a Saint
1 Samuel 16:7

I. **Our Distorted Vision**
   A. We look on the outward appearance of things
      1. We judge people by their outward appearance
      2. We judge circumstances by what they seem to be
   B. We may view this death in a distorted way
      1. We may see it as a terrible tragedy
      2. Tragedies are often victories in disguise
         a. Example—the crucifixion of Jesus
         b. Example—the death of a saint
      3. Tragedies can be growing experiences
         a. Job and his suffering—Job 42:3
         b. The death of a loved one

II. **Our Distorted Values**
   A. God looks on the heart
      1. He is more concerned with character
      2. He is more interested in eternal things
   B. We give little attention to these
      1. We grieve over injury, scarring, and death
      2. We are hardly moved at all by spiritual tragedy
         a. Neglect of church, Bible study, prayer, etc.
         b. Failure to accept Jesus as Savior
   C. These should be our first concern—Matt. 6:31–33

III. **Our Departed Friend**
   A. How should we feel about this death?
      1. We should not think of it as a tragedy
      2. We should see it as a victory—1 Cor. 15:57
      3. We should rejoice over the good life lived
   B. How should we face the days ahead?
      1. We should expect to follow the departed—Heb. 9:27
      2. We should glorify God in our lives—1 Cor. 10:31

8

A Good Man
1 Samuel 25:1

I. Good People Are Not Excused from Death
    A. ''Samuel died'' is a universal statement
        1. Death is the end of all earthly life (plants, animals, etc.)
        2. Death should not be a surprise to any of us
    B. Death comes to those of every race and nation
        1. The young, old, black, white, male, female, etc.
        2. The good are not exempt from this experience
            a. Lazarus, Stephen, James, and even Jesus died
            b. Death is not a penalty for being bad although it came as a result of sin

II. Good People Are Lamented at Death
    A. ''All the Israelites lamented him''
        1. Because of his life—his contribution
        2. Because of his death—his leaving
    B. Mourning is a natural reaction to death
        1. The bad and the good are both mourned
        2. Good people are mourned for two reasons
            a. Because of the life they lived—their contribution
            b. Because of their passage from our company

III. Good People Are Honored in Death
    A. All the Israelites gathered to honor Samuel
        1. He was honored by the presence of friends and family
        2. He was honored by recalling his good deeds.
            a. John the Baptist—Matt. 11:11
            b. Dorcas—Acts 9:36–39
            c. We mourn the deceased today
    B. The Israelites buried Samuel at Ramah
        1. They accompanied him to the graveside
        2. We will be accompanying the deceased today
        3. It is part of our expression of respect

9

Heroes of the Lord
Psalm 3:1–6

I. People Often Feel Helpless – vv. 1, 2
  A. Because of the multitude of their enemies
    1. We see our enemies as poverty, sickness, death, etc.
    2. We really have only one enemy—1 Peter 5:8
  B. Because of the apparent strength of our enemies
    1. The psalmists' enemies bragged that even his God couldn't save him
    2. We all feel this way at times

II. People Are Never Hopeless – vv. 3, 4
  A. Our hope is in the Lord himself
    1. Notice the word *but* in verse 3
    2. The Lord has never failed one of his own
  B. Our hope in the Lord is a total hope
    1. Physical hope—"shield"—protects our body
    2. Emotional hope—"head lifter"—beats discouragement
    3. Spiritual hope—"cried to"—settles the soul

III. People Are Sometimes Heroic – vv. 5, 6
  A. There are many kinds of heroes
  B. The Lord's heroes are unusual
    1. They are sometimes weak and sickly
      a. They often have thorns in the flesh as Paul
      b. They are sometimes seen hanging on a cross
    2. They are heroes because they endure
    3. They are heroes because they trust in God
  C. The Lord's heroes are sustained
    1. Sleep gets us beyond difficult times in life
    2. Sleep of death gets us beyond difficult transition from this life to the next

10

Life Takes Its Toll
Psalm 3:5

I. Our Friend Has Laid Down
  A. The time comes when our bodies wear out
      1. We are as the trees that grow in the forest
          a. They grow tall, strong, and healthy
          b. Age, insects, and disease take their toll
      2. We are as a car with many miles on it.
      3. We are as the flowers that grow in the field
          a. They begin as bulbs and grow to full bloom
          b. They wither and die in time
      4. We are as a fabric often worn
  B. Our friend continued as long as he could
      1. Time and disease weakened his body
      2. The time came when he ''laid himself down''

II. Our Friend Is Asleep
  A. The Bible compares death to sleep
      1. Lazarus was said to be sleeping—John 11:11
      2. Sleep is used three times in 1 Thess. 4:13–18
  B. You have seen the deceased sleep before
      1. We begin sleep fitfully but then it becomes deeper
      2. We observe something similar at death
  C. When he slept, we knew he was resting

III. Our Friend Will Awaken
  A. There is newness of life after sleep
  B. The Bible promises an awakening from death
      1. It is called resurrection—1 Cor. 15:19–23, 50–52
      2. Our friend will soon awaken to new life

IV. Our Friend Was Sustained
  A. The psalmist's enemies were seeking his life
      1. Sleep comes hard under such circumstances
      2. David put his trust in the Lord
  B. Our friend had put his trust in the Lord
  C. If we trust in the Lord he will sustain us.

16

11

Elderly Man
Genesis 25:7–10

I. Life Is Generous to Some People
  A. Abraham lived a full life—good old age
    1. Some are not given this much time
    2. The quality of life is more important than quantity
  B. The deceased lived a full life—good old age
    1. He gained much experience and wisdom
    2. He witnessed much history in the making
    3. He had many opportunities to do good—Gal. 6:10

II. Life Is Limited for All People
  A. Abraham gave up the ghost (died)
    1. Death is the separation of the body and spirit
      a. The body ceases to function
      b. The spirit goes to God—Luke 23:46
    2. Death is a change of status—1 Cor. 15:50
  B. All of us must face death sometime
    1. It is appointed unto all—Heb. 9:27
    2. Life should be lived with this in mind

III. Life Is Honored by Our Loved Ones
  A. Isaac and Ishmael buried their father
    1. Abraham had made some prior arrangements
      a. He had purchased the field of Ephron
      b. He had become a "friend of God"—James 2:23
    2. Abraham was buried with Sarah his wife
    3. Abraham was buried by his family
  B. We are gathered here to honor the deceased
    1. He had expressed some preferences
    2. It is fitting that his family has come to bury
    3. All of us need to make peace with god—Rom. 5:1

12

One Who Has Suffered
Psalm 25:15–18

Is there any virtue in suffering?

Anything to be learned from distress?

Anything to be gained from anguish?

I. **In Our Trials We Cry unto the Lord**
   A. This is a common human reaction
      1. Jonah cried "by reason of"—Jonah 2:2
      2. Hannah prayed "look on the affliction"—1 Sam. 1:11
      3. David pleaded—Ps. 25:18
   B. This was the reaction of the deceased I am sure
      1. God didn't heal and raise him up
      2. God enabled him to face death confidently
   C. God always hears and answers the afflicted—Job 34:28

II. **How Does God Answer Us in Our Trials?**
   A. Our relationship to God changes when we suffer
      1. When we are well there are conditions to be met
         a. There are things God wants us to do
         b. There are changes God wants us to make
      2. When we are suffering things are different
         a. Our ability to do some things is removed
         b. Our ability to make some changes is lost
   B. Notice how God deals in affliction
      1. "The Lord hath heard thy afflictions"—Gen. 16:11
      2. "I have seen the affliction"—Exod. 3:7
      3. God hears our affliction instead of our words
         a. Many times Jesus was moved by conditions not words
         b. God is moved by our state of affliction
      4. God responded to the deceased afflictions
         a. He gave peace of mind and spirit
         b. He gently helped to the other side

18

13

Remember
Psalm 39:5, 6

I. Remember Life's Destination
   A. The psalmist prayed to know his end—(v. 4)
   B. The Bible tells us every person's end
      1. We are appointed to die—Heb. 9:27
         a. Every person of past has died except two
         b. The grave is our understood destination
      2. We are bound for the judgment—Heb. 9:27
         a. All must give account to God—Rom. 14:12
         b. All must appear before the throne—Rom. 14:10
         c. No person needs to be unprepared

II. Remember Life's Measure
   A. Life is measured by time—days and years
      1. Each day therefore is a priceless treasure
      2. The rich would give all for one more day
   B. Life must be lived day by day
      1. We must live each day to the fullest
      2. We must fill each day with the best
   C. The days that make up our lives are all good
      1. God saw that it was good—Gen. 1:3-5
      2. Let us rejoice and be glad in it—Ps. 118:24
      3. Let us be thankful for the days of the deceased

III. Remember Man's Frailty
   A. Our bodies are susceptible to death
      1. We are prone to injury and disease
      2. We never know when the end will come—Prov. 27:1
   B. We should be prepared at all times
      1. By making sure of our salvation—1 John 5:12
      2. By walking in fellowship with God—1 John 1:7

14

A Father
Proverbs 4:1–27

We do not say all we would like to in life.
If this father could speak to his children today. . . .

I. Seek After Wisdom—(vv. 5–7)
   A. Wisdom has a starting place—Prov. 9:10
   B. Wisdom about life is the principal thing—(v. 7)
      1. We should desire it above all else
      2. The pearl of great price—Matt. 13:46
      3. Desire must precede possession
         a. Seneca: ''A large part of good is the wish to become good.''
         b. Jesus: ''hunger and thirst''—Matt. 5:6

II. Walk Not in the Way of Unrighteousness—(vv. 14, 18, 19)
   A. There are two ways open to all—Matt. 7:13
   B. The way of the wicked is as darkness—(v. 19)
      1. It is dark in its origin—Rev. 16:10
      2. It is dark in its course—Rom. 13:12
      3. It is dark in its destination—Matt. 8:12
   C. The way of the just is as a shining light—v. 18 (1 Cor. 13:12)

III. Keep Your heart with All Diligence—(vv. 23–27)
   A. Guard your heart with all caution—(v. 23a)
      1. Do everything to keep it pure—1 Peter 3:15
      2. Avoid everything which corrupts it—v. 24 (Rom. 12:2)
   B. Out of the heart come the issues of life—(v. 23b)
      1. Condition of heart determines kind of life
      2. Out of it come things which defile—Matt. 15:18–20
   C. Ponder the path of your feet—v. 26 (Ps. 119:105)
   D. Seek those things which are above—Col. 3:2

15

Comfort for God's People
Isaiah 40:1

In times like these, we look for comfort.

I. There Is Comfort Available
- A. Grief sometimes refutes this
  - 1. Severe grief can defy all comfort—Gen. 37:35
  - 2. Acute grief will refuse comfort—Ps. 77:2
- B. God's word to us is ''be comforted''
  - 1. The promise of God's Word—Isa. 66:13
  - 2. The power of God's Word—Mark 4:39

II. There Is Comfort in God
- A. We often look for comfort in the wrong places
  - 1. We look to man—Ps. 118:8
  - 2. We look to empty wells—2 Peter 2:17
    - a. Empty wells of religion and philosophy
    - b. Empty wells of psychiatry and astrology
    - c. Empty wells of pills and alcohol
    - d. Empty wells of work and activity
- B. We should look to the Lord—Isa. 51:12
  - 1. He comforts those who seek comfort—Isa. 61:2
  - 2. He comforts those who are cast down—2 Cor. 7:6
  - 3. He comforts in tribulation—2 Cor. 1:3, 4
  - 4. He comforts those who mourn—Matt. 5:4
  - 5. We should rise out of our grief and come—Mark 10:49

III. There Is Comfort for God's People
- A. God's people are special in his affection
  - 1. He has a special love for them—Ps. 149:4
  - 2. He calls them to comfort—text
- B. God's people receive special care
  - 1. Special care in life—John 11:10
  - 2. Special care in death—John 14:1–3

16

The Way of Death
Isaiah 42:16

Children ask questions about death.

Adults ponder about death.

I. The Way Is Unknown
   A. We don't know what it is like to die
      1. It is ait—Josh. 3:4
   C. We can face death confidently—Ps. 23:4

II. The Way Is Prepared
   A. The Lord promised to prepare the way for Israel
      1. To make darkness light before them
      2. To make the crooked things straight before them
   B. The Lord has prepared the way for us
      1. He has provided a plan of salvation
         a. He gave his only begotten son—John 3:16
         b. He calls us through the gospel—Rom. 1:16
      2. He has prepared a resurrection—1 Cor. 6:14

III. The Way Is Secure
   A. The Lord's promises in the text
      1. I will bring them—his power
      2. I will lead them—his guidance
      3. I will not forsake them—his loyalty
   B. The Lord's promises apply to us
      1. He will bring us to heaven—John 14:3
      2. He will lead us through death—John 10:27, 28
      3. He will never forsake us—Heb. 13:5
   C. Written in flyleaf of Bible:
      Lay any burden upon me, only sustain me;
      send me anywhere, only go with me;
      sever any tie but that which binds me
      to thy service and to thy heart.

17

Reasons for Confidence
Isaiah 43:1

God's people have confidence in death.
Note three reasons for this confidence.

I. **God Has an Investment in Us**
   A. He has redeemed us—Isa. 62:12
      1. He has bought us back—Rev. 5:9
      2. He has paid the price to reclaim us—1 Cor. 6:20
   B. He has redeemed us without gold—1 Peter 1:18, 19
      1. The price was the blood of Jesus—Rev. 5:9
      2. This investment puts a premium value on us
         a. Value is determined by the amount paid
         b. Value is determined by heart attachment

II. **God Has a Knowledge of Us**
   A. He knows our name—John 10:14
      1. Wrangler knew thirty horses by sight and name
      2. God knows every one of his children personally
   B. He knows our circumstances
      1. He knew when Lazarus died—John 11:11, 14
      2. He is aware of your circumstances today
   C. He knows our need—Matt. 6:8
      1. He knew the need of the disciples—John 11:15
      2. He will supply your need—Heb. 4:16

III. **God Has Possession of Us**
   A. God says "Thou art mine"
      1. This is more than a relationship
      2. He guards his possession—1 Peter 1:5
   B. God takes care of his possession
      1. He preserves their souls—Ps. 97:10
      2. He protects their bodies—Jude 9
   C. Hymn: God Will Take Care of You

18

The Suffering Savior
Isaiah 53:4, 5

I. The Lord Suffered
   - A. He has suffered many things—Luke 17:25
     1. He was stricken, smitten, and afflicted (v. 4)
     2. He was wounded, bruised, and chastised (v. 5)
   - B. The Roman cross was a cruel death
     1. Death on the cross was dreaded more than any other form of killing
     2. Death on the cross involved much suffering

II. The Lord Suffered for Us
   - A. He bore our sorrows and grief (v. 4)
     1. He bore the grief you experience today
     2. He is able to comfort you today
   - B. He suffered for our transgressions and iniquities (v. 5)
     1. The just suffered for the unjust—1 Peter 3:18
     2. This was according to God's plan—1 Cor. 15:3
   - C. He was chastised for our peace (v. 5)
     1. For our peace with god—Col. 1:20
     2. For our peace with men—Eph. 2:14

III. The Lord Suffered for Our Healing
   - A. By his stripes we are healed (v. 5)
     1. He obtained physical healing for us
        - a. Physical healing through medicine
        - b. Physical healing through miracles
     2. He obtained spiritual healing for us
        - a. He invites us to come for healing—Matt. 9:12
        - b. He is able to save to the uttermost—Heb. 7:25
     3. He obtained eternal healing for us
        - a. The resurrection of the body—1 Cor. 15:42
        - b. The restoration of the environment—Rev. 21:1–4
   - B. There is healing for your hurts today—Matt. 11:28

19

Come to Jesus
Matthew 11:28–30

I. There Is Help in His Person—Come
- A. Children are summoned to their mother
  1. When they are injured, hurt, distressed, or upset
  2. To receive her soothing comfort
- B. Christians are summoned to their Savior
  1. When burdened and heavy-ladened (v. 28)
  2. To receive his soothing comfort—Isa. 49:13

II. There Is Strength in His Presence—Take
- A. Recall Jesus on the way to the Cross
  1. His burden was more than he could bear
  2. Simon carried the Cross—Matt. 27:32
- B. Sometimes our burdens are too heavy
  1. Jesus invites us to enter his yoke (v. 29)
  2. Jesus invites us to let him help (v. 30)

III. There Is Hope in His Knowledge—Learn
- A. What do we need to learn about Jesus?
  1. That he is meek and lowly in heart—(text)
  2. That he did not come to condemn—John 3:17a
  3. That he came that the world might be saved—John 3:17b
- B. What do we need to do about Jesus?
  1. Accept him as personal Savior—Rev. 3:20
  2. Discover that our hope is in him—Ps. 78:7, 8

IV. There Is Rest in His Invitation—Find
- A. The word *rest* appears twice in the text
  1. Jesus said "I will give you rest" (v. 28)
  2. Jesus said "Ye shall find rest" (v. 29)
- B. These promises have one condition
  "Come"

20

Death of a Child
Mark 5:21–24, 35–43

I. The Father's Prayer (v. 23)
  A. He prayed for the Lord to heal her
     1. This would be a parent's first reaction
     2. This man's plea grew out of his grief
  B. I am sure you prayed for God's healing

II. The Father's Hope (v. 24)
  A. Jesus accompanied the father
     1. The presence of Jesus always brought hope
        a. Mary and Martha—John 11:21
        b. The blind men—Matt. 9:27
     2. The father's faith was strengthened
  B. Jesus has not forsaken you today

III. The Father's Distress (v. 35)
  A. Word arrived that the child was dead
  B. Nothing can be more devastating
     1. The loss of a child is a terrible experience
     2. The words hurt like no other

IV. The Father's Challenge (v. 36)
  A. Jesus told him to believe and not fear
  B. We underestimate the person of Jesus Christ
     1. We underestimate his power—Matt. 28:18
     2. We underestimate his provision—1 Cor. 2:9
  C. Jesus calls you to believe and not fear

V. The Father's Joy (vv. 41, 42)
  A. Jesus raised the child from death
  B. Jesus will raise this child one day
     1. His words to Martha—John 11:25
     2. He is coming again—1 Thess. 4:16–18

21

Jesus at a Funeral
Luke 7:11–17

Funeral services are not a recent custom.

Each funeral has things in common with others.

I. **The Funeral Was in Progress**
   - A. The man was being carried out (v. 12a)
     1. They had completed the preparation
     2. They were on the way to the burial site
   - B. The service was well attended (v. 12b)
   - C. We are gathered today for such a memorial service

II. **The Lord Had Compassion on the Family**
   - A. He saw and felt their grief (v. 13a)
   - B. He spoke words of encouragement (v. 13b)
   - C. He stopped the funeral procession (v. 14a)
   - D. The Lord has compassion on you today
     1. He sees and feels your grief—Isa. 53:3
     2. He speaks words of comfort—2 Cor. 1:4
     3. He stands ready to heal broken hearts—Ps. 34:18

III. **The Lord Exercised His Power**
   - A. He commanded the young man to rise (v. 14b)
   - B. He delivered the young man to his mother (v. 15)
   - C. Some day the Lord will exercise his power again—1 Thess. 4:16–18
   - D. Someday this family will be reunited
     1. What a day of celebration that will be
     2. Recall men coming home from the war
     3. We all need to make preparations

IV. **The People Glorified God**
   - A. They said God had visited them (v. 16b)
   - B. Let us glorify God today
     1. Glorify him in our spirits—1 Cor. 6:20
     2. Glorify him in our minds
     3. Glorify him with our words

22

Go On Living
John 4:50

I. The Command—Go Thy Way
- A. He was saying to go on about your living
  - 1. He told the man to go back to his home and his life
  - 2. He would have said this to anyone—John 19:26
- B. Death causes some to stop living their lives
  - 1. They can't get past their grief and loss
  - 2. Jesus would say "Go on with your living"

II. The Promise—Thy Son Liveth
- A. Jesus promised the man a reunion with his son
  - 1. It had to do with the state of his son
  - 2. In this case it was a reunion in this life
- B. Jesus promises a reunion with the deceased
  - 1. We need to understand the state of death
    - a. It is described as sleep—Matt. 27:52
    - b. It is a temporary state—1 Thess. 4:16
  - 2. It is a reunion in the future
    - a. It is a reunion of the resurrected—1 Thess. 4:17
    - b. Think of the joy of that reunion

III. The Requirements—Believe the Word
- A. Belief involves mental acceptance
  - 1. It is agreeing with what is said
  - 2. It is approving of what is said
- B. Belief is also physical obedience
  - 1. The man went his way—he obeyed
    - a. This is a true sign of belief
    - b. Lot's sons-in-law didn't believe him
  - 2. Will you believe God's word today?
    - a. Will you invite Jesus into your heart?
    - b. Will you go on about your living?

23

Someone Who Cares
John 11:35

Shortest verse in the Bible says who did what.
This verse reveals the heart of God.
The context reveals much more—John 11:28b–45.
  Jesus cares what is happening to you.
  Jesus cares what you are feeling.

I. We Have Someone Who Can Feel Our Sorrows
   A. Other people don't always feel or know
   B. Jesus saw them weeping and groaned (v. 33)
      1. Isaiah called Jesus a "man of sorrows"
      2. Philip P. Bliss song: "Man of Sorrows"
   C. We are never alone in our sorrows

II. We Have Someone Who Can Share Our Suffering
   A. Jesus was sharing their suffering when he wept (v. 35)
   B. Some thought it was his love for Lazarus (v. 36)
      1. They wondered why he let Lazarus die
      2. We often wonder why our loved one was allowed to die
   C. Jesus enables for whatever he allows—Phil. 4:19

III. We Have Someone Who Can Carry Our Burdens
   A. Jesus said "Come unto me all ye that labor"—Matt. 11:28
      1. It is easier for two to pull a load than one
      2. Burdens are easier when a friend stands with us
   B. There is no greater friend than Jesus—John 15:13
      1. He is there no matter what the burden
      2. He invites you to cast your care on him—1 Peter 5:7

IV. We Have Someone Who Can Undo the Cause of Sorrow
   A. The cause was the death of Lazarus
      1. Jesus called Lazarus forth (v. 43)
      2. Jesus won the victory over death—1 Cor. 15:25
   B. The cause is the death of our loved one
      1. One day Jesus will say "Come forth"
      2. We have a promise—1 Thess. 4:16–18

24

Death of the Chosen
John 15:16

I. Christians Are Chosen
  A. We do not seek after God in salvation
  B. We are sought out by God in salvation
    1. Through the preaching of his Word
    2. Through the activity of his Spirit
  C. We are chosen by our response to salvation
    1. Jesus knocks at the door—Rev. 3:20
    2. We must open the door—Rev. 3:20

II. Christians Are Ordained
  A. Ordained to go to the world
    1. Bearing precious seed—Ps. 126:6
    2. Bringing people to Jesus—Matt. 28:18–20
  B. Ordained to bring forth fruit
    1. This is the measure of a life—John 15:8
    2. This is the purpose of life—John 15:2
  C. Ordained to bring forth lasting fruit
    1. The effects of our works continue after death
    2. The value of our works follows us beyond death—Rev. 14:13

III. Christians Are Privileged
  A. Privileged to have access to God
    1. Access to God in prayer—Heb. 4:16
    2. Access to God in person—Eph. 2:18
    3. Access to God in times of need—Matt. 11:28
  B. Privileged to have a relationship with God
    1. A relationship through Jesus Christ—John 1:12
    2. A relationship like father and child—Rom. 8:15
    3. A relationship like shepherd and sheep—John 10:14
    4. A relationship like vine and branches—John 15:5
    5. A relationship that overcomes the world—1 John 4:4
    6. A relationship that overcomes death—1 Cor. 15:57

25

What to Expect
Acts 24:15, 16

I. The Expectation—Resurrection
- A. We expect the dead to be raised
    1. Because of the words of the Bible—2 Cor. 4:14
    2. Because of the words of Jesus—John 11:25
- B. We expect the just to be raised (v. 15)
    1. To life everlasting with God—John 10:28
    2. To the rewards of the just—Matt. 25:21
- C. We expect the unjust to be raised (v. 15)
    1. To appear before the judgment—Rev. 20:11–15
    2. To account for the deeds of life—Rom. 2:6

II. The Exercise—Righteousness
- A. We should strive for a clear conscience
    1. A conscience void of offense toward God—(v. 16)
    2. A conscience void of offense toward men—1 Cor. 10:32
- B. We should try to live a good life
    1. A saved life—Ps. 40:1
    2. A secure life—Ps. 40:2
    3. A satisfied life—Ps. 40:3
    4. A surrendered life—Ps. 40:4
- C. We should seek after righteousness
    1. Our first concern should not be material—Matt. 6:25
        a. The example of the birds—Matt. 6:26, 27
        b. The example of the lilies—Matt. 6:28–30
        c. The Lord knows our needs—Matt. 6:32b
    2. Our first concern should be righteousness—Matt. 6:33
        a. That is the nature of God's kingdom
        b. God promises to supply our needs
- D. We should seek the person of God—Isa. 55:6
    1. He is near to you today
    2. He can be found if you will seek—Prov. 8:17

26

The Sufficient Jesus
Romans 5:10, 11

I. We Are Reconciled by His Death
   A. We had a problem situation
      1. Our sins had separated us—Isa. 59:2
      2. The prodigal son illustrates—Luke 15:13
   B. He had a perfect salvation
      1. He bore our sins on the cross—1 Peter 2:24
      2. He brought us back together—2 Cor. 5:18a
   C. Death is not going out to meet an enemy
   D. Death is going home to our Father

II. We Are Saved by His Life
   A. We are saved by his resurrected life—John 14:19
      1. He ever lives to intercede—Heb. 7:25
      2. He stands ready to receive—Acts 7:56
   B. We are saved by his exalted life
      1. He reclaimed his exalted position
      2. He reclaimed his eternal power
   C. We are saved by his triumphant life
      1. Saved from the hold of Satan—1 Cor. 15:25
      2. Saved from the hold of death—1 Cor. 15:55–57

III. We Have Joy Through His Person
   A. Joy in what God is
      1. He is love, mercy, and compassion
      2. He is truth, holiness, and justice
   B. Joy in what God has
      1. He has the whole world in his hand
      2. He has us in his possession—John 10:25–40
   C. Joy in what God does
      1. He lifts up the fallen—James 4:10
      2. He comforts the sorrowing—2 Cor. 7:6
      3. He strengthens the faltering—Ps. 27:1

27

Faithful Christian
Genesis 24:56

Words of Abraham's servant to Rebekah's family might be words of deceased to us.

I. Hinder Me Not
- A. This could mean two things
  - 1. I have had full life and am ready
  - 2. I have had a glimpse of heaven and am eager
- B. God creates a desire for heaven—Phil. 1:23

II. The Lord Hath Prospered Me
- A. The servant spoke of his purpose
- B. God has a purpose for every life
  - 1. The faithful have fulfilled their purpose
  - 2. The faithful give God the glory
  - 3. Paul finished his course—2 Tim. 4:7
  - 4. The departed finished his course
    - a. The plan has been carried to its conclusion
    - b. The servant has gone to his reward

III. I Go to My Master
- A. These are the words of a faithful servant
- B. What happens when a Christian dies?
  - 1. His body ceases to function
    - a. His world-consciousness ends
    - b. His body awaits resurrection—1 Thess. 4
  - 2. His soul continues to live—Luke 16:22
    - a. His self-consciousness survives
    - b. It is said that we always participate in our own dreams
  - 3. His spirit goes to be with God
    - a. His consciousness of God increases
    - b. Stephen—Acts 7:59
    - c. The thief on the cross—Luke 23:43
- C. Death, then, is going to be with the Lord

28

Unto the Lord
Romans 14:7, 8

I. The Christian's Life—unto the Lord

   A. If we live, we live unto the Lord (v. 8)

      1. We live to please and satisfy him—John 8:29

      2. We live to honor him before men—Matt. 5:16

   B. This is the purpose of life—Acts 17:28

      1. It is Christ living in us—Gal. 2:20

      2. It is our motivation—1 Cor. 10:31

II. The Christian's Death—unto the Lord

   A. If we die, we die unto the Lord (v. 8)

      1. Jesus in Gethsemane—Matt. 26:42

      2. Our attitude should be the same—Matt. 6:10

   B. If we die, we go to the Lord

      1. The thief on the cross—Luke 23:42

      2. The words of Paul—Phil 1:23

   C. If we die, we die in the Lord

      1. The blessed—Rev. 14:13

      2. The faithful—Heb. 11:13

III. The Christian's Position—We Are the Lord's (v.8)

   A. We belong to the Lord by creation

      1. Job's confession—Job 10:8

      2. The purpose of creation—Prov. 16:4

   B. We belong to the Lord by redemption

      1. We are his by purchase—1 Cor. 6:19, 20

      2. We are his by ransom—1 Tim. 2:6

   C. We belong to the Lord in life or death

      1. The Lord diligently guards his own—1 Peter 1:5

      2. The Lord anxiously awaits his own—Luke 15:20

      3. The Lord has prepared for his own—1 Peter 1:4

29

Never Failing Love
1 Corinthians 13:8

I. God Loves Us in Life
  A. He states it in his word
    1. What manner of love he has—1 John 3:1
    2. The truth of his love—1 John 4:10
  B. He shows it by his willingness
    1. His willingness to give his son—John 3:16
    2. His willingness to accept us—John 6:37
  C. He seals it with his presence—Eph. 1:13

II. God Loves Us in Death
  A. We see it in his provision for us
    1. His provision for our salvation—Rom. 5:6
    2. His provision for our souls—John 14:2, 3
    3. His provision for our bodies—1 Cor. 15:49
  B. We see it in his pity for us
    1. He pities like a father—Ps. 103:13
    2. He pitied Israel and carried them—Isa. 63:9
    3. He will carry you in love
  C. We see it in his presence with us
    1. The promise of it—Heb. 13:5
    2. The reality of it—Ps. 23

III. God Loves Us in Eternity
  A. Parents loving presence makes a home
  B. God's loving presence makes a heaven
    1. He will be there to love us
    2. He will be there for us to love
  C. God's love will exist after death
    1. It will be experienced forever
    2. It will be enjoyed forever
    3. God's love never faileth

30

Younger Person
James 4:13–15

I. **We Should Not Expect a Long Life**
   A. Many do live to a ripe old age
      1. Many Bible characters were "full of years"
      2. My father was 82, mother 79, grandmother 86, etc.
   B. Many enjoy good health for many years
      1. Elderly man died who had never been in a hospital
      2. More healthy old people today than ever
   C. We should not expect this for ourselves
      1. It is guaranteed to no one (v. 14)
      2. We are stewards of life—Luke 12:42–48

II. **We Should Make the Most of Each Day**
   A. Each day should be savored to the fullest
      1. As a delicious meal to be enjoyed
      2. As a delightful scene to be observed
   B. Each day should be wisely utilized
      1. It will not come our way again
      2. It will be called to account—Acts 17:31

III. **We Should Trust God for Each Moment**
   A. We should submit to God's will
      1. Seek his plan for our lives
      2. Seek his guidance for our path—Ps. 37:5
   B. We should trust God's wisdom
      1. God knows what a day holds—Matt. 24:36
      2. God knows what each of us needs—Matt. 6:8
   C. We should be about God's business
      1. His business must be our business—Luke 2:49
      2. Be not weary in well doing—2 Thess. 3:13

31

What Is Life?
James 4:13–15

I. Life Is a Brief Moment in Eternity
  A. James compared it to a vapor (v. 14)
  B. People always bemoan its briefness
    1. If one dies young, we say "What a shame"
    2. If one lives long, we say "It passed so quickly."
  C. Time is therefore our most valuable asset

II. Life Is a One-Time Opportunity
  A. Life should always be viewed as an opportunity
    1. An opportunity to do good—Gal. 6:10
    2. An opportunity to bless others—Matt. 25:40
    3. An opportunity to glorify God—Matt. 5:16
  B. Life is a one-time opportunity
    1. Whatever we are to do we must do now
    2. Each day is a day for action

III. Life Is a Period of Preparation
  A. What shall we be in eternity?
    1. What we have become in this life—Rev. 22:11
    2. What we are when we die
    3. This makes our manner of life important
  B. This suggests that there is life after death
    1. To prepare implies something in the future
    2. There must be a way to prepare for that something
  C. This brings us to the person of Jesus Christ
    1. We must establish a relationship with him—Acts 4:12
    2. We must willfully decide to receive him—John 1:12
    3. He is the way to prepare—John 14:2b–6

32

Rejoicing in Death
1 Peter 1:3–9 (TEV)

I. We Are Told to Give Thanks (vv. 3–5)
A. Because of God's great mercy (v. 3)
B. Because of God's great gifts (v. 3)
1. The gift of life that does not end with death
2. The gift of hope that extends beyond the grave
C. Because of God's great promises (vv. 4, 5)
1. The promise to keep our inheritance (v. 5)
2. The promise to keep us for our inheritance (v. 5)

II. We Are Told to Be Glad (vv. 6, 7)
A. This is a very big order sometimes
1. God never said "Don't be sad."
2. It is necessary to be sad (v. 6)
B. There is a purpose in trials
1. The example of gold being purified (v. 7a)
2. Faith must be purified through trials (v. 7b)
3. We should welcome trials because faith is more precious than gold
C. There are rewards for enduring (v. 7)
1. We shall receive praise, honor, and glory
2. We shall receive these at the coming of the Lord

III. We Are Told Why to give Thanks and Be Glad (vv. 8, 9)
A. Because we love God (v. 8)
1. Our well-being is first in his heart
2. He never puts more on us than we can bear (1 Cor. 10, 13)
B. Because we are receiving our salvation (v. 9)
1. We know where it is all leading
2. We know God is working out our salvation
3. Faith is not believing God can but that God will

33

Conduct in Mourning
1 Peter 1:6–9

I. Rejoice in Heaviness (v. 6)
  A. There are many burdens to bear
    1. Death is not the only burden
    2. Death may be the heaviest one
  B. We can rejoice in heaviness
    1. Rejoice that burdens are seasonal (v. 6)
      a. Preacher preached on "It came to pass . . ."
      b. The end of suffering is always near
    2. Rejoice that God is faithful—1 Cor. 10:13

II. Praise in Trials (v. 7)
  A. Faith is more precious than gold
    1. Gold cannot buy peace of mind
    2. Faith alone can give one comfort
  B. Faith is tried by fire
    1. "Tried" means put to the test
    2. "Tried" means purified and refined
  C. Endurance in trial honors God
    1. It proclaims his sufficiency—2 Cor. 12:9
    2. It proclaims his faithfulness—Phil. 4:19

III. Trust in Your Salvation (vv. 8, 9)
  A. Salvation is of God—Acts 1:11
    1. God has provided it—John 3:16
    2. God has offered it—Rev. 22:17
  B. Salvation transcends the death of the body
    1. It is called eternal—Heb. 5:9
    2. Death is not the end of life—Phil. 1:23
  C. Salvation guarantees the safety of the soul
    1. Our souls have an anchor—Heb. 6:19
    2. Our souls have a shepherd—John 10:9
  D. Salvation promises the resurrection of the body—1 Cor. 15:53

39

34

The Enduring Word
1 Peter 1:24, 25

I. The Flesh of Man Dies
  A. It is described as like grass (v. 24)
    1. All grass has its season—life span
    2. When the season is over it dies—withers
  B. Human flesh has its season—life span
    1. We call it "a lifetime"
    2. Every lifetime comes to an end—death
  C. This is the natural order of living things

II. The Glory of Man Fades
  A. It is likened to a flower (v. 24)
    1. The glory of a plant is its flower
    2. The plant is known by its flower
    3. The flower of a plant soon fades and dies
  B. It is the same with man's glory
    1. The glory of a man are his achievements
    2. The man is known by his achievements
    3. The achievements of man end at death
  C. Jeremiah's exhortation—Jer. 9:23, 24

III. The Word of God Endures
  A. The word of salvation endures
    1. It endures for every generation—Ps. 145:4
    2. It endures for all eternity—Isa. 40:8
  B. The word of instruction endures
    1. It is profitable—2 Tim. 3:16, Ps. 119:105
    2. It is palatable to the heart—Ps. 119:11
  C. The word of comfort endures
    1. Such as Psalm 23, John 14, and Rev. 21:1–4
    2. This is one of God's great gifts to man

35

Events After Death
Revelation 20:12

I. Standing Before God
   A. Everyone will stand before God
      1. Small and great—no exceptions
      2. They shall be gathered—Matt. 13:41-43
   B. Not everyone will stand to be judged
      1. Some will be spectators—the saved
      2. Some will be participants—the unsaved—Rev. 20:11-15

II. Opening of the Books
   A. There are at least three books mentioned
      1. Books—plural—at least two
      2. Another book—singular—makes three
   B. The one book is the Book of Life
      1. This one tells who has been saved
      2. This one lists those who have received Jesus—John 1:12
   C. The plural books are books of works
      1. These determine rewards and punishment
      2. These list the deeds done in life—2 Cor. 5:10

III. Judging of the Dead
   A. "Judge" means to make a determination
   B. There are two determinations to be made
      1. Whether or not a person has been saved
         a. Whether he accepted Jesus in his lifetime
         b. Whether he appropriated the atonement of Christ
      2. The degree of reward or punishment
         a. Nothing we do is ever forgotten—good or bad
         b. Every deed done will be judged—Rom. 2:6
   C. Death brings it all to a climax
      1. Our earthly opportunities are over
      2. Our eternal appointments are waiting
      3. What manner of persons ought we to be therefore?—
         2 Peter 3:11

36

Better Over There
Revelation 21:4

I. **The Cause of Human Suffering—Tears**
  A. The cause from a historical viewpoint
    1. The sinfulness of Adam—Rom. 5:12a
    2. The sinfulness of all men—Rom. 5:12b
  B. The causes given in the text
    1. It refers to death, sorrow, and pain
    2. These are common to all people everywhere
    3. These are dreaded by all people everywhere

II. **The Comfort of God's Ministry—Wipe**
  A. God is our source of help
    1. He will wipe all tears from our eyes
    2. He will wipe all grief from our hearts
  B. God's comfort is inexhaustible
    1. We can draw on it for all we need
    2. We can draw on it as often as we need
  C. God's hand is never withdrawn—Isa. 59:1
  D. God's eyes never close—Ps. 121:4, Deut. 11:12
  E. God's love never ceases—Heb. 13:5

III. **The Promise of God's Word—No More**
  A. We will not have to suffer over there
    1. There will be no more causes for it
    2. There will be no more occasions for it
    3. These things will all have passed away
  B. We will have new bodies—1 Cor. 15:51–54
  C. We will have a new home—Rev. 21:1, 2
  D. We will have a new schedule—Rev. 21:25
  E. We will have all things new—Rev. 21:5